"Don't strive to make your presence noticed, just live to make your absence felt!"

Congratulations!

Having Satisfactorily Completed The Requirements For

GRADUATION

Has Been Granted Admission
and a Full Scholarship to

"The School of Hard Knocks"

Effective immediately!

GRADUATION:

"So, What Just Happened?"

Words of Wit and Wisdom

Tom Swanson

aka "Professor OB1 Kaswanni"

SF
Simple Faith Books
Boise, Idaho

GRADUATION: "So, What Just Happened?"
Published by Simple Faith Books
www.SunriseMountainBooks.com
13347 W. Tapatio Drive
Boise, ID 83713

All Scripture quotations marked NLT are taken from the *Holy Bible*,
New Living Translation, copyright ©1996. Used by permission of
Tyndale House Publishers, Inc., Wheaton, Illinois. All rights reserved.
"The Christian Manifesto" by Lloyd Ahlem originally appeared in the
April 15, 1982 edition of *"The Covenant Companion."* Copyright ©
1982.by Covenant Publications. Reprinted with permission.

Because most of the one-liners in this book came from so many
unconventional sources over a period of many years, proper
footnotes are impossible. Many one-liners have been used so
frequently they have become part of the oral tradition and now are
archived in the wisdom of the common man. Attempts were made to
identify the origin of these sayings wherever possible. The author is
grateful for the original authors and speakers who shared their
wisdom and insights now recorded in this work, and will gladly give
credit in subsequent editions should the original sources be
identified.

Cover Image: archana bhartia/shutterstock.com. Licensed.
Cover Design: Marilee Donivan, Sunrise Mountain Books
Interior Design: Marilee Donivan, Sunrise Mountain Books

ISBN 978-0-9842362-8-2
First printing 2013

Printed in the UNITED STATES OF AMERICA

Acknowledgments

First of all, sincere thanks to all the authors and creators of all the one-liners I have used in this book. Most of them came from conversations with the common man. They have become part of the wisdom that helps lead so many in successful living. They have become a major part of the way I think and live.

My wife Donna, my daughters Kyna and Terry, and two dear friends Marilee Donivan and Judy Rasmussen, have encouraged me over many years to put my one-liners and words of wisdom in writing. Thanks for your long years of encouragement.

This book would not be possible without the personal and professional support of Marilee Donivan at www.SunriseMountainBooks.com. Marilee has not only provided wisdom and support in writing and publishing this book, but has been a personal friend with unending friendship, love and encouragement.

Dedication

with love, hugs, and thanks to:

My dear wife of 47 years, Donna Serena Swanson,

My daughters Kyna and Terry,

My grandchildren Caleb, Joshua, Alex, Ross, Tyler,
Samuel and Elizabeth,

All the students and athletes at Dansville, MI, Potterville,
Michigan; and at Lake Hazel Jr. High, Meridian High, and
Centennial High in Meridian, Idaho;

All the Young Life students and leaders from Capital
High and Meridian High in Idaho,

and the Young Life family in Russia, Ukraine, Armenia,
Moldova, Georgia, Uzbekistan, Kazakhstan and
Kyrgyzstan.

⁂⁂⁂

CONTENTS

A gift of wisdom to this year's Graduates
from Rudyard Kipling...

" If "

Source: *A Choice of Kipling's Verse* (1943)

If you can keep your head when others all about you
Are losing theirs and blaming it on you,
If you can trust yourself when all men doubt you,
But make allowance for their doubting too;
If you can wait and not be tired by waiting,
Or being lied about, don't deal in lies,
Or being hated, don't give way to hating,
And yet don't look too good, nor talk too wise:

If you can dream—and not make dreams your master;
If you can think—and not make thoughts your aim;
If you can meet with Triumph and Disaster
And treat those two impostors just the same;
If you can bear to hear the truth you've spoken
Twisted by knaves to make a trap for fools,
Or watch the things you gave your life to, broken,
And stoop and build 'em up with worn-out tools:

If you can make one heap of all your winnings
And risk it on one turn of pitch-and-toss,
And lose, and start again at your beginnings
And never breathe a word about your loss;
If you can force your heart and nerve and sinew
To serve your turn long after they are gone,
And so hold on when there is nothing in you
Except the Will which says to them: 'Hold on!'

If you can talk with crowds and keep your virtue,
Or walk with Kings — nor lose the common touch,
If neither foes nor loving friends can hurt you,
If all men count with you, but none too much;
If you can fill the unforgiving minute
With sixty seconds' worth of distance run,
Yours is the Earth and everything that's in it,
And — which is more — you'll be a Man, my son!

Work for a cause, not for applause.

Live life to express, not to impress.

Introducing...

"Professor OB1 Kaswanni" and His One-Liners

Since I am a long-time, world-class, professional procrastinator, how did **GRADUATION: *"So, What Just Happened?"*** come to be a reality?

First, writing a book was not my idea. Countless friends and former students, and Young Life kids have encouraged me to put my thoughts in writing. I've learned it's a lot more difficult for a talker to be a writer. Please forgive some of my amateurish style, just think of it as a grandpa having fun telling stories to his kids and grandkids.

A wise man never blows his knows in public.

I was checking out at a store with many checkout lines in Boise, Idaho. All of a sudden I heard a loud voice behind me, **"Don't be sorry, BEHAVE!"** *I turned around and a checkout clerk, who was a former student, said, "Thanks, Mr. Swanson, that one-liner has saved my life many times."*

INTRODUCING...

My fascination with one-liners began in junior high school. I was reading a bulletin board in the locker room and focused on a small 3x5 card. *Life is a tough teacher: first you get the test, then you get the lesson!* I was not taught that line: I learned it and have carried it with me the rest of my life.

Ideas "stick" when they "click"! All of your memories "clicked." All of your learning "clicked." You have replaced the "Oops, not again" with "AHA! ☺"

From 1975 through 1980 I had a class of students in Potterville, Michigan Middle School that were in my physical education class for their 5th through 8th grade year. I then moved to Idaho.

In 1984 they invited me back to speak at their graduation ceremony. I felt deeply honored. To see if any of my one-liners really did have any *"stickability"* after a four-year absence, I inserted ten one-liners into my talk.

I started my talk with some general comments of a sincere thank you, and words of congratulations. Then while just continuing to speak I used my first one-liner without any introduction, and stopped halfway through, looking down at my notes like I had forgotten the rest of the line. In a few seconds, someone somewhat timidly spoke up and finished the one-liner.

Proceeding without comment, two students piped up for the second one-liner. By the fifth or sixth time, students didn't wait for me to pause, finishing the line while I was still speaking. The audience was chuckling by the time I used the tenth one-liner.

INTRODUCING...

I then shared that students learn often without being taught. I had never used these one-liners in some academic, teaching situation. I just kept using them in conversation and interacting with students.

One-liners really do "*stick*", often because they really do "*click.*" Somehow in their minds, it just "*clicked!*" When something clicks in your mind it sticks! You don't have to work at learning it, you just do.

> *Steve was a football player in my freshman algebra class. Academic rigor was not his highest priority. His senior year he was cleaning out his locker, as I happened to walk by. He mentioned, "Coach Swanson, thanks for the conversation we had my freshman year when you said, 'If not you, who? If not now, when?' That line has really helped me. I will never forget you, or that line. Thanks!"*

A great source for my one-liner collection has been 35 years of high school yearbooks. I loved to see the one-liners each student chose.

There was no limit to the professors I have had at the **"One-Liner University."** Teacher in-services, coaching clinics, sermons, students, conversations, mom's wisdom, bulletins, grandpa's wink and wit, newsletters, restaurant placemats, billboards, reader boards, email copies, *Country* magazine, *The Reader's Digest*, and comics have all been instructors that helped produce the wit and wisdom gathered from, and for, the common folk. Many times a one-liner was written on a little piece of paper and given to me. Many thanks to the original authors.

INTRODUCING...

As we started driving, my very young grandsons, Caleb and Josh, said, "Grandpa's not buckled his seatbelt." Why? They had not heard the "click" of the seatbelt.

Clicking that leads to sticking is important. One-liners are unique and oblique, and help things "click" and "stick".

Be yourself! Everyone else is taken.

Every one of us is unique. Part of my uniqueness is my curiosity about how life works. What can be learned from the success of others? I guess I have a "how to" marker on my DNA.

Life can only be understood looking backwards; it can only be lived going forwards.

One-liners are my road map. My map helps me remember successful journeys, reminds me of bad trips, points out beautiful scenery, makes me reflect on fellow travelers, and sets up my future journeys. It helps me ☺. My hope is that you can reflect, renew and learn from my road map.

My map won't work for you: you must make your own. Pick and choose wisely those ideas that will help you grow, improve and mature. It is YOUR future. Enjoy your journey.

It's what you learn after you know it all that counts.

❖❖❖

 # "AHA!"

What's clicking and sticking?
Here's an "AHA!" page for your own one-liners!

Graduation: "So, What Just Happened?"

First of all, whether you have just graduated from day care, or received your Ph.D., congratulations are in order. Every step along your academic career is worthy of recognition. Job well done; another milestone accomplished.

Is commencement a celebration of finishing, or getting ready for the start of the next leg on your journey? The word "commence" really means to begin, or start. Even so, taking a moment to recognize significant accomplishments is a worthy pause before you get back on the road of life.

Life is often lived looking backward. Isn't the gift of memories fantastic? The people, places, events, joys, and lessons learned all make for a rich history. But, after a moment's reflection, I hope you realize you can't live there—your future awaits!

"So, what just happened?" Bad news can become good news. *"Losing is winning if it turns you around!"* [Bob Stromberg song]. Let's take a look at some of the implications of having reached this academic milestone. What's coming *next*?

Get ready. Your world will be changing. Growing up always has a way of bringing the new, interesting, different, and often challenging. When you reflect on the coming change, do you really want to spend your life riding your tricycle and playing in the sandbox?

Let's take a quick look at ten things that will be changing as you move on to the next chapters in your life. Whether you are going on to world of work or to further education, life will change. A little reflective anticipation is often worthwhile.

1. Structure: However your current world is organized, it will change. New is always different. *Growing up is optional, growing old is mandatory.* Keep reflecting on these topics.

2. Parents: To grow up, your parents will become a lesser influence on your daily decisions. As you move out into the world, you will have to make more and more of those daily decisions.

3. Teachers and Coaches: Those significant adults in your past have been a great gift to be treasured. The adults in your future will assume a different role.

4. Friends: Just like you, your friends will be moving on to their new chapters. When you reunite, they will have been changing and adjusting to their new lives. You are now on your own: *Don't be sorry — behave!*

5. Hometown: Life in the hometown and in your family will go on as you move to new locations for jobs and colleges. In a real sense, you can't go back home; it all will be continuing to change.

6. Church: Hopefully your upbringing has had a significant spiritual dimension. As you journey on in life, your church remains "back home." Will you continue, or will you seek out having a strong spiritual presence in your new chapters in life?

7. Choices: The factors that were a part of your decision making process will change. You're grown up now! Will the wisdom of your upbringing continue to be a part of your choices? *You will get one of two things in life — results or excuses!* You still have to live with the consequence of your ongoing choices.

8. Time: You will be in control of your time choices. Freedom has its own price. You can spend your time as you wish. Make your spending pay beneficial results.

9. Responsibility: You will become the driver of your life. With that comes the opportunity to do what you want. Accept it, and make good choices. *If not you, who? If not now, when?*

10. Opportunity: Wow! You have waited for this day. The future is yours. Go for it! *If you seek a helping hand, there is one at the end of your arm!*

"AHA!" SECTION 1

A big part of any "next step" experience is looking around at all the new faces that are now quickly becoming a major part of your new reality. One factor in the process is sizing up or comparing all these new folks. Wise evaluation and careful discrimination of important criteria is important.

It is best to start off on the right foot. *It is a lot easier to stay out of trouble, than to try and get out of trouble!* Slowing down, remembering your highest priorities will prove valuable in the long run.

You must also remain your realistic, best cheerleader in the process. It is normal to exaggerate other's qualities, and diminish your own qualities. Be encouraged, and encourage yourself daily, so that you can maximize this transition. Expect it to take some time.

While almost everything will appear new as you journey, remember you are the same person. As my dad wisely said, *"Be true to the best that you know."* Don't become a chameleon and try to adjust to every new person and situation.

As soon as you can, you should be developing your action steps moving forward. Build a realistic view of your new challenges, and make some preliminary short-term goals. *Then, remember to focus every day on your "New Day's Resolutions!"*

Going forward, it is your new world that is growing, expanding and developing. *To the world, you are a tiny part; to yourself, you are the world!* Proceed wisely, purposefully, and cautiously.

Life will appear to come at you very fast, even appearing to keep on gaining speed. You must choose to focus on the important, skip a lot of the unimportant stuff. *Your choice for today: whine, shine or recline!*

Looking back at your life should be encouraging. At each step of your life, you have successfully chosen and executed a winning strategy. You have graduated and moved on to your next challenges.

Be encouraged! You are totally capable of making good choices and accomplishing your goals. Validate yourself on past accomplishments.

"Life is difficult," is how Scott Peck started his best selling book,*"Taking the Road Less Traveled."* To accomplish worthwhile goals, it is wise to anticipate a great challenge. You can succeed, and it will be worth it!

Be encouraged! Expect to work hard and adjust to the realities of being an adult. You will learn quickly *life is so doggone daily!*

New experiences and challenges will produce new learning. You will have to add knowledge and skills to your tool bag for success. You have done it before; you can do it again. *"You can do it! Yes, You can!"* [World famous philosopher, Bob the Builder!]

You can't live the rest of your life in a moment: *Life by the yard is hard; by the inch, it's a cinch!* Break it down into day-by-day projects and enjoy the journey until your next commencement!

"AHA!" SECTION 1

Be encouraged! Anticipation is often the greater part of experience. I hope you are full of dreams and aspirations. It will take a lot of perspiration, coupled with significant inspiration, but you can climb your mountain of success. *Remember, nobody fell to the top of the mountain.* Enjoy your climb and safe travels!

Coffee Break!

"Let's Try Not To Strain Your Brain."

"Do not let fear confine your life
inside a shell of doubt.
A turtle never moves
until his head is sticking out!"
                    Charles Chigna

The mock turtle, in a deep hollow tone, said, "Sit down, and don't speak a word 'til I've finished."
So they sat down and nobody spoke for some minutes. Alice thought to herself, "I don't see how he can ever finish if he doesn't begin?"
                    Alice in Wonderland

There are two kinds of people who enter a room:
One says, *"Here I am!"*
The other says, *"Ah, there you are!"*

Patience: Putting up with those who you would like to put down!

He Who Laughs: Lasts!

So, Is it the End, or the Beginning?

Commencement is both a special day of celebration, and a day just like every other day. Every day is a new day to be lived in the active present tense. You can't live yesterday, and you can't live tomorrow. Make today count!

Your lifestyle mental set going forward is critical. Are you a member of the "hard work" or the "quick fix" mentality? Have you been snookered into believing there is an easy way to success?

> *"But doctor, I have problems trying to swallow pills," said the patient.*
> *The doctor responded, "Don't worry, that's no problem. I've got a pill to solve that, too."*

The other end of the spectrum focuses on hard work. ***"Most of the footprints on the road to success have been made by work boots!"***

Your lifestyle of behaviors and your worldview of your preferred future are in for a challenge. You will have to step up to the next level of opportunity and responsibility. Every commencement step is the start of your next chapter. Every day you will be writing your own personal success story.

> The little guy was really excited. His dad had asked him to go with him to the lumberyard, and help him buy some lumber. The little fella approached the desk and asked for twenty-four "4 by 2's."
>
> The man at the desk asked, "Don't you mean '2 by 4's'?"
>
> "What's the difference?" asked the little guy.
>
> "Nothing, it's just the way we measure lumber," was the reply.
>
> The little guy said, "O.K."
>
> "How long do you want them?" asked the man at the desk.
>
> The little guy proudly said, "Oh, we want 'em a long time; we're building a garage."

Think back to some of your early memories. I hope they are pleasant and enjoyable. But, commencement means one chapter ends and a new one begins. So, too, you must ramp up your expectations and evaluations. Expect to continue growing up in all areas of your life.

Do you remember the first time you got to use the family car entirely on your own? I remember a lot about that first time. What a feeling of independence.

Be encouraged! I hope you are excited about your next steps. Anticipation needs to be based on reality. Success must come in a reality-based world.

Since commencement is also a start in your next educational experiences, let's do a quick little activity about your past and future learning.

1. Fold your hands like you are praying.
2. Unlock your fingers and switch them all with your other thumb on top.
3. I bet it feels different and weird.
      ****That's just like life:
      new behaviors feel different!
4. Cross your arms.
5. Now cross your arms the other way.
6. I bet you had to think about it, often trying several possibilities.
      ****When learning new things,
      you have to think about it.

Managing your feelings, taking them into account, but NOT being driven or controlled by your feelings is a major growth step. Using a train analogy, feelings are a terrible engine but a useful car in the train. Rational decision-making considers emotion as only one minor part of a major decision.

The old axiom that practice makes perfect reminds us that nothing is ever learned and perfected the first time. Repeated, correct practice will improve our knowledge and skill over time. Typing or keyboard skills are a great example. You don't start out typing 100 words a minute.

Focused attention to the process of mastering any skill will pay great dividends. *Wherever you are: be all there!* Intense concentration on the task at hand is a trait to be mastered!

Be encouraged! Remember frequently to pat yourself on the back. Having graduated into the next step, you bring with you a successful package of knowledge and skills preparing you for this next step. *Just be careful not to break your arm patting yourself on the back too hard!*

You must learn to control your intensity and energy on your journey. Develop a well thought-out plan of attack. *Plan the work, then work the plan.* Know what you're doing, and keep checking your progress.

A word of caution: *activity is not always productivity!* It is very normal to get so excited about reaching the top of your mountain, you get lost in the buckwheat. Consider:

> *The task at hand was to cut a trail through the jungle. Within minutes, the project started, and progress was steady.*
> *One smart fellow climbed to the top of the tallest tree. The word came down from above, "Wrong jungle!"*

Rudyard Kipling in his fantastic poem "IF" states: *"If you can keep your head when everyone around you is losing theirs, and blaming it on you!"* [*Professor OB1 encourages you to memorize that poem.*] Keeping your cool is a skill well worth perfecting. Controlling your emotions and operating rationally should become a lifelong operational goal.

Reality based "will power" must become your traveling partner. Keep developing your road map, goals, and action steps. Frequently remind yourself: *"Perfect aim is useless unless you pull the trigger!"* A smooth and steady combining of your plans and the process will produce your best chances of continuing progress. Refining your expectations into a thoughtful timeline will keep you "truckin'" along. Slow and steady now!

Develop the ability to prioritize your daily calendar. Breaking big projects into manageable tasks will help you keep your composure. Don't expect to perfect the skill immediately, so master the flexibility skill.

In the next six "AHA! Insights," let's look at some ideas that will assist you on the immediate tasks at hand. *An ounce of preparation is worth a pound of cure!* I know you are excited, but you will benefit from some calm reflection.

Knowing who you are, where you are starting from, and getting your mind prepped will pay great dividends. Further down the highway of life, you will look back and compliment yourself on being well prepared before you took off on your journey.

Be encouraged! Put the one-liners in your mental backpack for ready reference. *One-liners "click" and help wisdom and truth "stick!"* They will become your best traveling companions, frequently reminding you to adjust and keep on track!

"So, What Just Happened?" will become a quick reference guide for quick "pick me ups", and "I almost forgot" type of moments. It is a great encouragement to know where to turn for friendly advice.

So, as you step out and begin the next phase of your life's journey, give thanks to William Safire of the New York Times:

"Stop putting second things first!"

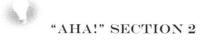 **"AHA!" SECTION 2**

Once again, be encouraged! You are well prepared for continuing on your journey. *Talk soft, talk hard, but don't scold yourself!* Focus every day, and enjoy your trip. Take note of your fellow travelers and give them a word of encouragement. We all need each other. Carry on!

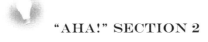

Next!

The most important thing you do in life is what you do next!

Interesting, but very true! What we do next is the only thing possible. We are always living forward!

It would be most beneficial to be doing those next things based on wisdom and some forethought. If instant impulse is your automatic response, anticipate some surprising results. Better to have run your response through your best decision-making process.

Now you find yourself between the past and the future. You have a much better understanding looking backward. Hope you possess a wealth of wisdom, knowledge, and experience heading into your "next" steps.

Some folks get stuck in the past and present, unsure or afraid of going forward. You will never be perfectly prepared for the "next" step. Willingness and courage need to move you onward.

Be encouraged! As you have successfully navigated your life this far, your lessons learned have prepared you for your next steps. Practical accomplishments are your goal, not perfection.

If you don't expect to make mistakes, don't expect to make anything!

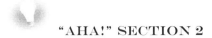

Cognito Ergo Sum

Never let the facts get in the way of a good theory!

"Cognito Ergo Sum" is a dictum coined in 1637 by René Descartes, who is sometimes called the father of modern philosophy. This phrase is his conclusion on building a life philosophy. His starting point was, "I think, therefore I am".

So, what is your starting point? It is my belief that somehow we have to pound a nail into the wall to start hanging our life on it. We have to define a starting point and move forward from there.

A meaningful life has to be more than running around in circles, chasing rainbows. Why are you alive, and what are you trying to accomplish in your life? Where are you going, and how do you want to be remembered?

The root meaning of education is "to lead out from." As you process life, you *are* moving out from somewhere every day. Does your direction have a destination and purpose?

Be encouraged! Everyone will not be moving in the same direction and at the same speed. YOU decide what is beneficial and meritorious for you, and just "keep on truckin'!"

Now that my mind is made up, don't confuse me with the facts.

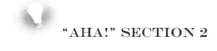

The Main Thing!

The Main Thing is to Keep the Main Thing, the Main Thing!

My pastor, David Roper, introduced me to this idea. He shared about searching for a new wristwatch when his old faithful one had died. In jest he said the new watches tell you everything except the actual time.

So, what would you say is *your* main thing? I'd encourage you to check your day timer and your checkbook. Where do you actually *spend* your time and money?

My brother gave me a t-shirt for my 40th birthday: "The older I get, the better I was!" It is challenging to accurately qualify and quantify yourself. Coming to understand our "main thing" takes honesty, humility, and courage.

Proving the congruency of triangles is a big part of my geometry class memories. Developing congruency in our lives proves equally challenging. Do we consistently live out what and who we desire to be in our best thoughts and moments?

You are encouraged to get reflecting and refining YOUR main thing. My journey keeps returning to: "For me to live is Christ and to die is gain." [Philippians 1:21] Keeping the main thing the main thing is a worthy challenge and goal.

We are drowning in information, while starving for Truth.

Self Help

If you seek a helping hand, there is one at the end of your arm!

Approaching the bookstore's information desk, the clerk was asked, "Where is the self-help section of your store?" The clerk look puzzled, thought for a moment and responded, "If I told you, wouldn't that defeat the purpose of your search?" Self-help is self-help, or is it?

Personal curiosity and responsibility are commendable. A big part of navigating this life successfully is being assertive and getting things figured out. While seeking wise input, you have to do the "putting it all together" yourself.

Everything does not have to be your own invention and creation. There are lots of excellent examples and models to consider. *All of us are smarter than any one of us.*

It would be wise to consider the wisdom of the ages during your search. Old isn't always bad, and new isn't always good. You will be blessed, or cursed, by your selections, so choose wisely and implement well.

Be encouraged! There is a reason for considering the "Wisdom of Solomon." The Bible has stood the test of time, offering wisdom and *salvation* for generations. You don't have to start from scratch and reinvent the wheel.

"Wisdom is skill at living." [David Roper]

20 Letters: 10 Words

If it is to be, it is up to me!

"Yo, I get it!" While I might not like it, I get it. Why should I count on anyone else, or want anyone else to be living MY life?

It might prove a little scary, or intimidating, but I would not want it any other way. It is empowering to realize that I can and must be in charge of living my life. I am the only person who will spend 100% of my future with me!

Now the reality sets in. First reflect briefly on some of the important lessons from your past. Next, analyze realistically your present situation. Then become strategic and dynamic in moving on into your immediate future.

As a young driver, my dad gave me some valuable insight. If you don't want some responsible adult riding shotgun for your driving career, you better accept and demonstrate that mature responsibility in driving your car and your life. HUGE thanks, Dad!

Be encouraged! A great attitude, focused effort, and "stick-to-it-ness" will get you a long way down your highway of life. It will take daily considerations, but you can keep building a meaningful future for yourself.

Don't let what you CAN'T do, stop you from doing what you CAN!

School of Hard Knocks

"too soon old, too late smart"

The cartoon showed a professor in a top hat standing under a sign advertising, "Professor so-and-so's, School of Hard Knocks." The professor was giving a kid a kick in the fanny, while saying, *"I don't care if you're not one of my students. Get your fanny into class!"*

Enrollment and daily attendance in the school-of-hard-knocks is mandatory—for life! No use whining about it being too hard, or "not fair!" You have no options but to show up every day.

Learning the lessons of life is also mandatory. You will learn! Applications of those lessons are your choice, but if so, relearning those lessons will automatically be repeated.

It would be in your best interest to apply your learning immediately. You will be the one who benefits. Why not be nice to yourself and have an improved future?

Be encouraged! Mandatory enrollment in the School of Hard Knocks can turn out to be really helpful. You already have paid the tuition, so why pay twice to learn the same lesson?

Two wrongs don't make a right;
two Wrights make an airplane!

Coffee Break!

"Let's Try Not To Strain Your Brain."

> Why are we such a jealous guardian
> of the humility of others?
> John Powell,
> *The Secret of Staying In Love*

"The worst disease that any human being can
ever experience is that of being unwanted.
Except there are *willing* hands to serve and
hearts to love, I don't think this terrible disease
can be cured."
Mother Theresa

"...when the saints go marching OUT!"

Jeff Kemp was a NFL quarterback. Jeff said it
didn't matter that much if he could throw the ball
90 yards at 80 miles an hour. It didn't matter that
much if he could read the defenses perfectly and
avoid the rush. While they are important, the
single most important skill for a quarterback was
to get the ball to the receiver "so it was impossible
for him to not catch the ball." The pass must be
"receiver-friendly."

He Who Laughs: Lasts!

So, What's Different about Today?

Either you enjoyed all the fuss made about graduation, or maybe it was a little overdone. Were you uncomfortable being the center of attention? Whatever your response was, all that is now history.

Now it is the proverbial morning after the night before. The pressures to jump all the hurdles, and go through all the hoops to successfully navigate the graduation trials are now over. You are one day closer to freedom, and being on your own. *Finally!*

Mom couldn't quite understand what the little guy was doing. He was up early, seemed more organized and determined than normal. She was really baffled when he made a bag lunch, got his winter clothes on and said, "Have a great day Mom," and went out the front door.

She peeked through the front window unnoticed. After what seemed a fairly long time, the little guy came back through the front door.
"Mom, where does Daddy go when he leaves every morning?"

Be encouraged! Today is another day to go out the front door to the world of the big people. Hopefully, you've dreamed and anticipated this day coming, and now it is here. The fantasy of your younger years is over, and the new reality has arrived. Right on time!

Hopefully, you noticed the admission document inside the front cover of this book. You have been admitted to the *"School of Hard Knocks."* Expect to have many "nobody told me so" experiences. The learning curve will bend increasingly steeper.

It will be impossible for you to anticipate everything you will experience in your new future. You have observed much of the real, adult world. The lesson to be learned from observing is far different from participating in the real world.

While praying for a good harvest: HOE!

But as we say in the Idaho mountains, *"Cowboy Up!"* Today must be lived and experienced as a brand new day. Today's test will produce today's learning.

Much of your life has been spent being part of a family, school, church, team, or hanging with your "best buds." First of all, much of that has to change, as you most likely will be in new and unfamiliar surroundings. Welcome to another difference about today.

48

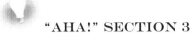

Be encouraged! While you are about to learn some lessons about "aloneness" as you become more and more "on my own," Don't think, good or bad, like or dislike, right or wrong, it just is; and you must adapt and adjust to your new reality.

I remember a conversation with my dad about driving my own life on into the future. He asked if I preferred my parents to continue riding "shotgun," and being a constant part of my life-long journey. Another lesson learned.

It is a normal rite of passage that you desire to become independent and not "have to obey" your parents. It is a healthy development, but there is a price to be paid when you become "free at last." You should not expect to be independent, and still expect your parents to pay the bills.

Make tomorrow's dreams today's energy!

Be encouraged! Keeping your excitement and anticipation of your optimistic future in check, emotional self control must keep improving. Learning to channel that positive energy into constructive action steps is what it will take for success. Slow and steady wins the race!

Just like the rabbit race with the tortoise, the wasted energy of the rabbit's flights of fancy led to his downfall. *Keep your eye on the prize!*

Emotion and feelings can be your source of useable energy, or become your worst enemy. *Once again your "will" must overcome your "wander"!*

You have loaded, and keep refining, the information entered into your mental GPS system. Those are your goals, so keep focused and encouraged. Start and end each day with a focused evaluation of your progress and tweak your next day's adjustments.

The most valuable thing in your bag of tricks is your attitude.

As you come to the end of the day, tomorrow already approaches. As you evaluate today's successes and lessons learned, it will seem that you never get a chance to enjoy the present. Success will come when you learn is not "either/or", but handling the "both/and" well.

Most choices are not like a true/false test, but more like multiple choice. The secret of doing well on multiple choice (or multiple guess) tests is to first eliminate the worst choices. The wisest of folks will then seek to consider all the best choices, even some they have not yet identified.

So if you plan to fail and succeed,
which have you done?

Be encouraged! You face a very serious choice: will you influence your world, or will the world influence you? There are a wide variety of both positive and negative influences you will have to consider. You must decide to proactively influence YOUR world for the good and best.

Many of those negative influences will come from other travelers on their journeys that have no interest in your success. They will use people [you and others] to accomplish their purposes. Your people-evaluating skills must keep improving and be up to the task.

The internet is another source of concern. The web can be a fantastic source of valuable information and a tool to be used to achieve your successful and worthwhile goals. It also can be a tremendous time waster and an unending cesspool of evil and destruction. Make wise choices, and be true to the BEST that you know!

People skills are rapidly changing in this world of smartphones, emails, and high tech developments. Remember the importance of your people skills, both in relating to you, and in relating to others. It is a different, quirky world, but love people and use things, not the other way around.

Be encouraged; that being said, it is a fantastic time to be alive. You can enjoy a healthy lifestyle where you can succeed a make a significant difference. As my dad encouraged me: *"Be true to the BEST you know!"*

The adventure begins where the road ends!

Now you have graduated and "commenced," ending the last segment of your previous adventure, and now you begin your next adventure. Accept it with enthusiasm; it can be "fantabulous!"

Adventure does not know what is over the next hill, or around the next curve. You have chosen this road, believing it will take you to your chosen destination. Every road contains the surprising and the unknown, both of which you must successfully navigate.

The Living Bible has a verse with a very instructive word in it. Hebrews 12:1 encourages the followers of Jesus to *"run with patience the **particular** race that God has set before you."* It is very insightful that you are running your "particular" race. So run it well with everything you have.

It probably will be congested and confusing as everyone is running his or her own unique and oblique journey. Prioritize your focus to your journey. Be friendly and encouraging, but while they are responsible for their journey, so are you. Pray, focus and be encouraged.

You must be your own "lead dog" on your journey. While all those loving and caring family and friends are "barking" their encouragement from behind, your "teammates" are expecting you to keep leading your "particular" race.

The scenery only changes for the lead dog.

So, what's different about today? It's a new day, full of adventure and responsibility. In the past you might have waited for direction from your parents, teachers or coaches. Now, it is your opportunity and responsibility to take charge, get focused, and take off into new territory.

Be encouraged! You are ready. Be confident of your own problem- solving abilities and your committed friends. You are ready!

🐾 🐾 🐾

Nobody Told Me!

"Making your way in the world today, takes everything you've got!" [Cheers Theme Song]

Have you ever watched a game or activity where you had no idea what was going on? Everyone is playing hard, no confusion, they understand the game, and are having a great time. Reminds me of Alice in Wonderland.

In life we start growing up and everything is new. Some of us have been blessed with wonderful teachers and guides—our parents. At some point we start to become independent and want to start living our own life.

The prodigal son in the New Testament is a classic story. The young fella gets to the point where he comes to the conclusion: "I want mine, and I want it *now!*" Ready or not, here I come!

Being an observer in life is a lot easier than being a participant. There is little consequence being an observer. Just push the replay button and do it over. Being a participant in life, you will learn some harsh lessons from Professor Reality!

Immaturity often responds with blaming the world with, *"Nobody told me."* Successful folks always approach the new with a curious willingness to learn. Humbly asking the successful participants in life the secrets of the game usually proves beneficial.

There is none so blind as one who will not see.

On Your Own

"Remember, Pilgrim, there is no path;
the path is made by walking." [Paula Ripple]

The time has now arrived. All those times you hoped you could just do it your way is here. More and more, you *will* be on your own.

With that awareness comes personal responsibility. No more finger-pointing and blaming. You decide, you do, it is now all on your shoulders.

You also control more and more of the decision-making. Less and less it will be, "What do you think?" You still are encouraged to seek wise counsel and input, but you alone have the final decision to make and implement.

Expect those days where you are a little *"whelmed."* Making your own path will be full of ups and downs. Keep a long distance view of the finish line, while you make step-by-step progress.

Be encouraged! You are taking a major step into adulthood. I hope you welcome this change. Becoming proactive in building your path to success is a sign of maturity.

Doing the right thing is easier
than explaining the wrong thing.

Free At Last

Whatever your lot in life,
build something worthwhile on it.

Freedom is a very unique and oblique word. Little kids understand it to mean life is an all-day play day. Go-anywhere-do-anything day with no adult hassle.

A more mature understanding points out your have both the freedom of choice, and at the same you are choosing the probabilities of consequences. Freedom does not live in the world of fantasy. Real choice means real costs, real benefits, or real consequences.

Freedom also presents the excitement of opportunity and possibility. With freedom comes the chance to explore and discover all kinds of interesting things. You can wander and search out those things that really interest you.

Mature discipline must be a part of your pursuit of freedom. Wisdom will teach you many lessons the hard way without emotional and intellectual discipline. Wandering aimlessly will get you lost.

Be encouraged! Freedom can be a tremendous energizer. This is what you wanted to pursue, *so go get it.*

My biggest problem is apathy, but who cares!

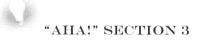

Anticipation

Nobody said it would be easy.
They said it would be worth it.

It has been said that anticipation is often the greater part of experience. *How do you keep your mind from wandering when you are day-dreaming?* It is easy to get lost and stuck in the fantasy world of anticipation.

Anticipation can be a solid motivator. You have clarified your vision and built an action step plan of accomplishment. Your excitement can be your power source.

It is easy for your mind to get off track and you end up at the finish line of your dream. *"YooHoo! You're not there yet; get back to work!"* Discipline your mind to keep you focused on making the anticipation into reality.

Tap into the power of your anticipation. Visualize you are succeeding, but temper that with an intelligent management of the trip's time line. Compliment yourself on the progress you are making.

Be encouraged! It is all coming together. Managing the step-by-step progress will turn your anticipation into reality.

Do not adjust your mind;
the fault is with reality.

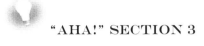

Choices

The ultimate reality in life is choice!

There have been many studies on how folks survived extreme hardship, torture, and punishment. One powerful conclusion is those survivors chose to focus on *"making it!"* They believed no one could take away their personal choice of how to respond.

When you are faced with something new, unexpected or challenging, it is valuable to focus on your first thoughts and feelings. Instant reactions and thoughts are revealing. How you choose to deal with those instant reactions will determine your success.

Take a few deep breaths, count to five, and then count to five again. Intelligent, rational self-talk is paramount. Calm your self down, and flip the careful consideration switch on in your brain.

No one else can make a choice for you of how to respond unless you give him, or her, that power. Continue to build *your* decision-making model. Take out your pad of paper and do your serious considerations on paper.

Be encouraged! We often center on worst-case scenarios, when we need to rationally consider all the options and consequences. Calm the urgency with well thought-out responses.

Quit blaming your boots
for the fault of your feet!

The Driver's Seat

If you don't have time to do it right the first time, when will you have time to do it over?

I know I did it. As a little kid most of us would sit behind the steering wheel, twist and turn the wheel, make "varoom, varoom" sounds, push the buttons and handles, pretending to be the driver. We couldn't wait to grow up.

In many ways, that day has arrived. Not only do you have a real driver's license, you have graduated to driving your own life. With freedom comes opportunity and responsibility.

A major part of driving is the process of getting safely from one place to another. Driving implies movement, hopefully towards a destination. You are the operator of that process.

You have already learned, now with significantly more parts to the process, that problem-solving and decision-making are a major part of your success. *You want it; you got it!* Drive safely and productively.

Be encouraged! Participating in the real driving world is an amazing experience. Millions depart and safely arrive at their destination. So can you!

A lack of planning on your part does not make it an emergency on my part!

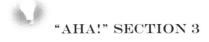

Coffee Break!

"Let's Try Not To Strain Your Brain."

A chaplain who went through the WWI invasion of Normandy on D-Day told me: "Before the invasion, the men respected me. After I had been with them on the beaches, I was one with them."

Leighton Ford

The Good Lord gave us two ears and one mouth, so we should listen twice as much as we talk!

Ideas for my next 3 books:
1- "Humility and How I Attained It!"
2- "When You've Got It, Flaunt It!
3- "You, Too, Can Be Cool!"

It takes a long, long time to make an old friend!

He Who Laughs: Lasts!

So, Are You Ready?

Ready? Isn't this an interesting word and concept? I was curious what the dictionary would say: *"prepared for immediate use."* My immediate response was, *"prepared for what?"* If you don't know what's coming, how can you be ready?

Exactly! You will never be perfectly prepared for every eventuality you might face in life. Whether it be knowledge, emotional maturity, skills, material supplies, or whatever, don't burden yourself with the perfectionist's definition of "ready." **Until you know, you'll never know for sure.**

A more practical understanding would be, are you ready for the challenges of life? Now, that is something you can enthusiastically embrace. You bet I'm ready! Bring it on! Let's see if I can battle that monster!

Be encouraged! Readiness is more of a willingness and attitude to face squarely the next challenge in life. It will always be somewhat surprising. Having that mindset prepares you to be at your best competitive readiness, anticipating, and equipped with a problem-solving expectation.

"Every bird must whistle through its own beak." [Ken Olson]

A 360-degree sense of awareness is being ready "for whatever," and will keep you on your toes. Don't burden yourself with worry. Deal with stuff when it arrives on the scene.

The key is to *respect the process*. Readiness is an ongoing process, not a singular event. You get better at being ready. Forget being perfect. Focus on being effective. Remember how you learned the foot pattern—right, left, right, left? Build from the basics and keep anticipating.

What does it mean to be effective? Quickly perceiving and building understanding of what it is you have to deal with is the beginning of effectiveness. You quickly figure out what is happening so that you can evaluate, strategize and implement.

Look on the back of any over-the-counter medicine. Tucked in there somewhere is the "active ingredient," the chemical that makes the medicine effective.

In being ready, *you* are the active ingredient. You have the greatest effect on the outcome. You control your self-talk. You are the decision maker, the executor of your choices. You must anticipate, face reality, finalize your choices, and make things happen.

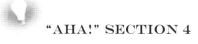 "AHA!" SECTION 4

Depending on your age and experience, always be open to wise and expert advice. Often having another few opinions and insights will help you bounce ideas around. All of us are smarter than one of us.

Do what you can, with what you have, where you are.

In life, simple reality determines that you are you! What happens and comes your way, is the unique and oblique developing story of your life. You have to help yourself max out and last for the rest of your life. Keep on making it a great story!

Be encouraged! Your wisest starting point is self-acceptance. Realistically, it's the only possible choice. You are who you are. Be good to yourself. Recognizing and accepting your starting point helps you on your way to empowering your effectiveness. You always must start from where you presently find yourself.

Having taught photography for many years and having taken thousands of pictures, I was often asked, "What is the best camera?" What camera takes the best pictures? My answer never changed. Cameras don't take pictures, people do! A camera is only one of the tools available. You are the operator.

Life deals you your hand of cards; you must play them!

Wisdom and skill need to temper your readiness. Life will keep teaching you lessons that only Professor Experience can teach. At this point in time you can only use the experience base you now possess. Continue to be the best student you can be.

Maintain a lifelong hunger for learning from the best professor, Experience. As a former wrestling coach, I taught each wrestler to be constantly aware of his position, and the opponent's present position. Then try to strategize to keep improving his position while your opponent is doing the same thing. Mental quickness and effective action will produce the winner.

The uniqueness of being a wrestler is that every wrestler is on his own, and has only his mental and physicals skills to match wits with his opponent. It is a valuable training ground to build individual responsibility. *If not you, who? If not now, when?*

Improvement begins with "I."

"I" is a most interesting word. Without ego strength, you will face a very challenging life. You must be assertive, advocating and executing your best efforts to succeed. With too much ego, you will also face a very difficult life. We all know of those "know-it-all" folks, who often try to push and bully their way to success.

Effective people skills focus on loving people and using things, not the other way around. You will have to develop your own strategies on dealing with pushy and overly aggressive, demanding personalities.

He who laughs, lasts.

Maintaining a light-hearted spirit, having a sense of humor, is important. Anger, intensity, and bitterness destroy your calm, creative, problem-solving thinking. You will have a lifetime challenge of effective emotional control, trying to find a balance between advocating your position, while not being over-powered by the aggressors.

Through trial and error, experience will continue to prepare you for the next challenges and opportunities for success. Developing good habits is beneficial, but every new situation requires fresh thinking, planning, and action. Resist automatically falling into relying on your habits from past successes.

Habit is the easiest way to be wrong — again!

Stephen Covey in his best selling, *"The 7 Habits of Highly Effective People"* says, "Habit is the intersection of *knowledge, skill* and *desire.* Knowledge is the *what to do* and *why*, skill is the *how to do*, and desire is the *want to do."* [p.47]

That describes the life-driving process. All three must be proactively processed. It all happens in your head before it happens in your life. Keep polishing and improving your entire problem-solving skills and habits. Improve your self-talk. Effective habits will help maximize your journey through life.

Unfortunately, other people will always be a part of your life. Be very thankful for dear friends, but be prepared for those "other kind" of folks. You will surely come across those over-opinionated folks who know everything about everything. You will find that they have all the answers to your situation, even without being asked. Keep this thought in the back of your mind so that you can smile.

Some folks don't have a clue; they don't have a clue!

Be encouraged! Strong thoughts, dynamic action and honest evaluation will give you your best chances of success. While being open to others, *you* remain the driver on your life's journey. You want to end up at your destination, not theirs.

A wonderful memory with my young grandson Josh was when we went to hear a very famous American philosopher. His words of wisdom: ***"You can do it! Yes you can!"*** [Bob the Builder]

Growing up before the TV age we played a ton of outdoor games. While playing hide and seek, the one who was "it" had to count to 100, and then yell in a loud voice, *"Ready or not, here I come!"* Just like that, *"ready or not"* life will be coming at you.

**If you don't know where you are going,
you are at the mercy of those who do!**

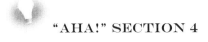

Live Ready!
You are breathing and have a pulse, but are you fully alive?

"Live Ready!" will seek to reflect on the process of being fully alive. An ancient philosopher said, *"There are as many opinions as men."* You will be presented with challenging thoughts to help shape your conclusions on being "fully alive."

I have often wondered what it means for someone, anywhere in the world, on any day in history, to wake up and face the day. What were they anticipating? What were they hoping to happen?

As the days pile up and run into each other in your memory, what new things in your life are you expecting? Is there something new you are hoping for today? *All of your evaluation starts with your expectations.*

How well defined are your destinations on your journey through life? Where are you heading, and what progress are you making? My prayer is that your life is purposeful and that you are making satisfactory progress.

It is hubris to think we are totally self-made, insulated against the ideas, opinions, and influence of others. We are the sum total of countless ideas, experiences, and responses. *"Live Ready!"* anticipates being a positive catalyst in the process of producing "fully alive" friends.

If you don't know where you are going, you will probably end up someplace else! Laurence J. Peter

67

For What?

Life is what happens on your way to somewhere else!

"Live Ready!" almost automatically implies *"For What?"* Life is not a single, still photograph, but is more like a movie or video, automatically recording how we live until some point in the future. We wonder where we are going; what really can we control?

Do you sometimes feel it would be easy to live someone else's life? Does your life ever seem confusing and not so easy? Everybody else looks like they "have their stuff together!"

At some point in your life, I hope you wake up and realize you are in charge of your life and your future. You didn't sign up for this life and didn't have much input for much of your present reality. But now you had better get on with living your life!

Be encouraged! At some point you start getting serious, and wonder where everyone is going. Everyone seems to be going in varying directions, following all kinds of different rules. Who decides how this game of life is to be played?

"Live Ready!" seeks to help you think through the complexities of life by giving interesting and insightful questions. YOU ultimately DO have the opportunity and responsibility to lead your own life. You are encouraged to accept that reality eagerly and cheerfully.

Life usually arrives early, and unannounced.

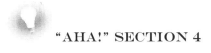

Alfie

"What's it all about Alfie— is it just for the moment we live?"

The movie *Alfie*, from the mid '60's, told the story of a young self-absorbed man. The above line comes from the movie's title song, which had a profound influence on this young college kid. Really, what is life all about?

Socrates, the ancient Greek philosopher was right on target: *"The unexamined life is not worth living!"* Either we answer the question for ourselves, or we become some kind of a puppet controlled by a mysterious puppeteer. How assertive are you in defining your life's journey?

The challenge, and opportunity, is to sort through the numerous voices clamoring for your attention. There are a plethora of advocates, from some "snake oil salesman" to voices of virtue. With the electronic world of the internet, the number of temptations increases exponentially.

Be encouraged! You are in charge of your choices. It is your life and, like many before you, you can find and live a meaningful life, finding blessings for others and yourself.

You must learn to say "no!" to much you come across in order to say "yes!" to the most important things. Become your own best cheerleader. It's your life, and you are making daily choices to produce your personal history and legacy.

The grass might be greener on the other side of the fence, but you still have to cut it!

Home Alone

I'm not OK, you're not OK, but that's OK!

Fantasy is a lot of fun. The original *Home Alone* movie was fantastic entertainment. You kept waiting for Kevin to pull another "fast one" on the robbers.

In an interesting way, you are "home alone." You have to realize and analyze your situation and come up with satisfactory solutions. That's part of your grand adventure.

Ready or not, you are in the middle of your story. Learn from your past, and off you go. You might not be facing "robbers," but you will be facing your own adventure.

There are major benefits in being home alone. It's your home, with the freedom and possibility of making it your special place. It will become the "home" of your pleasant and positive memories you are building.

Be encouraged! Protect your home turf. Keep all the unpleasant stuff of life out, and make yours a place of safety, security, and blessing.

Remember, that way you won't forget.

Aloneness

*Consider the mosquito: he doesn't get
a pat on the back until he gets to work.*

I hope you have some fantastic memories of doing things with your special friends. Family and friends make sharing life's experiences a wonderful time. Continue to invest in those special friends that travel with you on your life's journey.

A serious part of maturing is learning to accept and cherish the special uniqueness of being you. Learn to become comfortable in your own skin and being your own best friend. You will spend 100% of your future with yourself.

Being a strong and purposeful you is important. Self-confidence, but not arrogance, is a very positive character trait. Making a positive success story out of your life is noble.

You have the choice of being your own cheerleader or critic. Self-evaluation is valuable, only if it encourages and builds you into a better, stronger person. There are many sad stories of self-destruction.

Be encouraged! Cherish your alone times, celebrating the loving, caring person you are becoming. I hope you enjoy your own company, for you will be spending a lot of time together.

A mosquito doesn't wait for an opening—he makes one!

I'll Figure It Out!

When life gets hairy, shave!

In a certain way, "I sure hope you will figure it out!" That will become one of the major factors in you having a successful, enjoyable life. You *must* become successful by realizing, identifying, and solving problems in life.

Being a history major in college, my most memorable lecture was on the "tinkerers" who just kept monkeying around until they perfected their inventions. The talent and skill of figuring things out really is a gift. Hopefully your goal is to find solutions.

Horse sense is what keeps horses betting on humans. Common sense is a big source of figuring things out. It often is not mysterious or complicated.

Your fellow travelers are a great source of insight, wisdom, and experience. One magic word is *ask!* Share your solutions and lessons learned. We are all in this thing called life together.

Be encouraged! The great majority of folks have figured life out. Yogi Berra, the New York Yankee catcher, said something like, *"You can see a lot just by watching!"* ☺

Same behavior: same results.

Coffee Break!

"Let's Try Not To Strain Your Brain."

"A journalist had spent considerable time doing a story on the children of India. The overwhelming reality of the problem produced a cynical attitude in the journalist. When asking Mother Theresa how she planned to feed the needy children of India, she quietly answered, *"One at a time!"*

Coffee: Industrial Strength Break Fluid

Lead By Example
[Author Unknown]
I'd rather see a sermon than hear one, any day.
I'd rather one should walk with me than merely show the way.
I can soon learn how to do it, if you'll let me see it done.
I can watch your hands in action, but your tongue too fast may run.
All the lectures you deliver may be very wise and true,
But I'd rather get my lesson by observing what you do.
Though I may not understand you and the fine advice you give,
There's no misunderstanding how you act and how you live.

He Who Laughs: Lasts!

So, Where Ya' Headin'?

Well, it's about time! You are getting serious and excited about "getting on with getting on!" All this thinking and reflecting has given you a headache. The time is at hand to implement your action steps.

> *Remember the postage stamp secret of success:*
> *stick to one thing until you get there.*

It is most important to maintain a balanced approach between strong thought, dynamic action, and honest assessment. It's like the analogy of the three-legged stool—you need all three legs. Accept the wisdom of the ages; you don't need to reinvent the wheel. Accept reality and use that wisdom and energy to your advantage.

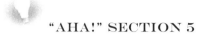

Your mature preparation over all these years will be of great benefit to you as you move out on your journey. It has not been wasted effort. It might be worthwhile to reflect on some of the goofballs and knuckleheads you have met on your journey. Be thankful for your wise decision-making and focused, hard work.

Take a serious interest in where you are going;
that is, where you will spend the rest of your life!

I really have tried to apply a thought I heard as a high school kid: **Using today wisely is the best preparation for tomorrow.** Life really comes down to the sum total of how you have used the days that have already passed.

Be encouraged! You are not stuck in a "today" time freeze. It is just the first day in the rest of your life: a great new day of possibility and opportunity. You can keep getting your act together and improving your daily effort and focus. Don't beat yourself up over perfection. Keep making each day count, one day at a time.

Knowledge is power,
vision is the steering wheel,
wisdom is the accelerator and brakes.

Hopefully, you have chosen intelligent destinations and made adequate preparation for your journey. If you are using someone else's plans, please reconsider if *you* will be happy and satisfied, especially when you arrive at where you are going. You have to live your own life.

"AHA!" SECTION 5

Life is *not* linear! Very seldom does one experience a perfectly smooth journey. Don't be surprised by speed bumps, potholes, flat tires, detours, weather problems, and a little road rage from those nasty fellow travelers. You have only yourself to blame for your speeding tickets.

Becoming upset and frustrated are common reactions, but a serious waste of time and energy. Productive self-talk is a fantastic traveling partner. Focus on solutions and get moving on your journey.

Don't beat yourself up when you make a wrong turn or get lost. Remember you are traveling in new territory and going on to a new destination. Humbly realize your situation, make corrections and keep moving in the right direction.

Effective leaders lead themselves first.

Emotional self-control is always a character trait that needs continuous adjustment. Expect stress and frustrations, it is part of the price of reaching out to bigger challenges. If it were too easy, it probably wouldn't be worth your effort. You have set high goals for yourself.

A good mental picture is to think of yourself as a thermostat instead of a thermometer. Expect to set the tone and temperature around you instead of adjusting the feeling-tone of your situation. Learn to deal with every variable you can control in your life with a constructive manner.

A critical insight says that it is impossible to know, or anticipate, exactly what your satisfaction factor will be at reaching your destination. We all have been disappointed with reaching your destination. We all have been disappointed with a gift or purchase when we have overestimated what we wanted. Remember:

Success is getting what you want;
happiness is wanting what you get!

While on your journey, you must score high in the "remembering" category. As I used to tell my students, the definition of forget is "choosing not to remember." One of my favorite grandpa memories is when Josh gave me the look and said, "Grandpa, I'm choosing to remember!"

Having a remember strategy will prove extremely valuable. Big projects, with big goals are far too complicated to just rely on your memory. You will need to develop a calendar and other detail tracking strategies.

Expect the critics and skeptics to come alive. You will find that this is the identity of some folks. Remember: *"The dogs will always be barking: that is all they do!"* Simply validate yourself, your efforts and your vision. You are the one who will reap the benefits of your success.

Really, does it matter what "they" think?

Along your journey, you will have interruptions, and you will have to take care to get all the other stuff done that life brings you. Expect to live a stop and start life style. I laughed the first time I heard: *"Have you ever stopped to think, and then forgot to start again?"* I have to seriously remind myself to get back

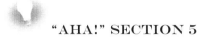

on track. I have learned that I am easily interrupted and distracted.

Understand that others will probably have little concern for the progress of your journey. Their travels are most likely their full time concern. *"If you won't budge, don't expect a nudge."* The world is often indifferent and will hardly notice if you are active or making progress.

Initiative, especially self-initiative, is a "must-have," and more importantly, a "must-do" on your part. Being a self-starter and a go-getter is mandatory. Remember, it is your plan, your journey, and your success.

*The winners are determined not at the starting line,
but at the finish line!*

Keep this picture in mind: *A turtle never goes anywhere without sticking his neck out.* Remember how we learned that you will never be perfectly prepared for your journey? Get started, build your momentum, solve problems as they arise, and "keep on truckin'!"

Just as while traveling you need "potty stops," expect to take needed breaks, rest, get prepared for the next leg, and get back on the road to success. It is intelligent planning to take mini-celebrations when you reach important plateaus. Treat yourself to a smile frequently. You are making progress.

Go as far as you can; from there you can see further.

Be encouraged! Learn to enjoy your journey. You most likely will be traveling for a while. Hopefully, you prize your

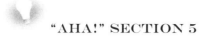

work ethic and your problem-solving skills. Remember to empower your resolve to complete your journey.

Life is lived in day-tight compartments. It would be sad to arrive at your destination and have no pleasant memories of your journey. Being always preoccupied and possessed by your journey is not the way to travel. Take a moment to stop and smell the roses on your travels.

You will never succeed on your own. Recognize all those partners and fellow travelers. Give them a pat on the back and say, "Thanks." *Life is too serious to be taken too seriously. Remember, he who laughs, lasts!* Safe travels, and carry on!

The only person to get his work done by Friday was...
Robinson Crusoe.

Destinations

If you don't know where you are going, any road will get you there!

"Hey! Where are you going?" Is your answer, "I don't know, I'll figure it out when I get there!"? Ready or not, life keeps coming at you.

At some point in our life, it should dawn on you that you have the opportunity and responsibility, to figure out where you are going. At first, the thought probably is a bit scary. Becoming overwhelmed is a common response.

We very quickly realize that life cannot be lived in freeze-frame. We must keep moving, or we'll surely get run over. We are forced to figure things out on the move, often going much faster than we would prefer.

Every culture postulates about ultimate destinations. Not only do we have to figure out where we are going in this life, but everyone else seems to have eternity (what happens when our lives end), already figured out. Whoa, I just got up and don't even know what I'm having for breakfast!

While you have the freedom to choose your destinations and how you want to travel, whom you ask for advice becomes paramount. You don't have to learn everything by your own experience. There are wise, informed folks who care about you, who have the *best* information to help you safely end up at *your* desired destination, both in this life and the next!

"If you're riding a dead horse, for Heaven's sake: DISMOUNT!" [Dr. Barry Asmus, Book Title]

Signposts

*A signpost needs to be in the right place,
with the right information,
pointing in the right direction.*

The news told of a lost hunter. When asked if he had a map and compass, he was asked why he didn't use them. He replied, "I didn't believe the compass!"

Traveling along our journey of life, it is best to have our destination firmly in our mind. Being an old driver education instructor, I usually made the final drives such that students had to plan their routes. A key part of success was knowing the "check streets" just before they had to turn.

Determining success in life often rests on how quickly we realize we have made a mistake, and how fast we can correct it. Signposts are those mental markers guiding us or correcting us on our journey. Knowing those signposts is crucial.

Some folks beat themselves up with perfection. There are few perfect journeys through life. Adapting, adjusting, and correcting make for a successful journey, so be thankful for signposts to help you on your way.

Life can be abstract, unique and oblique. It will take wisdom, skill, insight, and tour guides. Who we ask, what we choose, what we believe, and how we carry it out will become our signposts for a successful, productive life.

If you're lost, for Heaven's sake, keep driving!

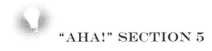

Process

Life is a journey, not a destination.

Process is a key understanding on your way to success. How long is now? Really, is there such a thing as now?

Process is the on-going essence of life. Breathe and walk are two examples of process. It is something you automatically keep on doing and doing.

Just like now is the indefinable passing point of the past turning into the future, so is process an ongoing activity. Using and maximizing process to your advantage is the key. Effectively partnering with constructive process is a skill to be mastered.

Just like riding a bicycle, you must keep moving forward. It has been said the learning curve of life is often very steep. Learning to ride the moving process is a skill you already have had a lot of success with, to have reached this point.

Be encouraged! Getting this far in the book and in your life shows you are mastering the ongoing process. Keep enjoying the movement, and keep adjusting toward success.

Today is the first day of the rest of your life.

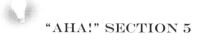

Your Life Equation

Formula for understanding teenagers:
(Energy without control) X (Velocity without direction)
X (Desire) X (Desire) = Teenagers

Having taught algebra for many years, it was always interesting when students asked for help. I always posted the answers, while they had to show the correct solution. I would usually follow their process, stop and point.

Most students would see their mistake without my saying a word. Often they would make some wrong calculation. Frequently they realized they had just forgotten, or dropped one factor in the process.

The first step is to choose the right equation for the specific problem. In life, that becomes very challenging. Often we don't have the learning or the experience to make the successful application of all the details.

Just like copying your neighbors work in math class, so it might turn out in life. You both might be wrong. It's best to get the best information, from the best sources, and make successful application of all the details.

In your life equation you will somehow put it all together. One factor you will choose to include, or omit, is the God or Jesus factor. You will have to decide if your successful life equation will need an eternal input and perspective.

There are only two things we can give our children: one is roots, the other is wings.

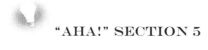 "AHA!" SECTION 5

Sounds Good

There is a significant difference between a good sound reason, and a reason that sounds good!

Every message and conversation contains feelings. We want to feel smart, to feel correct, to feel successful. There is trouble ahead if your conclusions are weighted towards good feelings.

Successful living contains "paying the price." It will take strong thought, dynamic action, and honest evaluation to reach the top of the mountain. Getting to the right destination requires countless decisions and safe, correct execution.

"When the going gets tough, the tough get going!" Temptation often challenges our decision-making. There must be, and there really is, an easier way. *Not so!*

Many fables are based on taking the easy way out. Our feelings can convince us that *"it's ok"* to choose plan B. "It sounds so convincing!"

Hindsight is 20/20 vision. *Learn from the experiences of others—don't be the other!* Wisdom and truth are based on good, sound reasons, not on reasons that sound good.

Experience is a tough teacher; first, you get the test, then you get the lesson!

Is the World Ready for Me?

Many live by the speedometer, instead of the compass.

I sure hope you are "cranked," "jacked," or whatever the word is that best describes your excitement about your future. Your mind-set, and self-talk will be a big part of your success. Your optimistic attitude and engaging personality will be of great help.

If that energy level indicates arrogance or obnoxiousness, watch out! It is very difficult to achieve lasting success by being too pushy, or a bully. You must always realize you live the real world of people, so maximize your effective people skills.

You must have enough "moxie" and self-confidence to choose to pay your entry fee and get prepared for the race of your life. Your determination to make your life matter by accomplishing your goals must be the starting point. You are motivated to become a mature, contributing, successful adult.

No need to apologize for your ego strength. As Tom Brokaw stated, *"It is a lot easier to make a buck, than make a difference."* It's OK to both make a buck and a difference, but you have to start taking those first steps on your journey.

Be encouraged! You have arrived at the "rocket launch" of your journey to success. The world is ready for you, and ready to congratulate you on your success in life.

If you make a mistake, don't follow it up with an encore.

Coffee Break!

"Let's Try Not To Strain Your Brain."

Coffee: Prepare to meet your maker!

A little boy was waiting for his mother to come out of the grocery store. As he waited, he was approached by a man who asked, "Son, can you tell me where the Post Office is?"

The little boy replied, "Sure! Just go straight down this street a couple blocks and turn to your right."

The man thanked the boy kindly and said, "I'm the new Pastor in town. I'd like for you to come to church on Sunday. I'll show you how to get to Heaven."

The little boy replied with a chuckle. "Awww, come on... You don't even know the way to the Post Office."

> "A friend is one who walks in when others walk out."
> Walter Winchell

The greatest gift we can give:
the <u>purity</u> of our attention!

He Who Laughs: Lasts!

Graduation: "So, What Just Happened?"
Words of Wit and Wisdom

Tom Swanson – *"Professor OB1 Kaswanni"*
38 Rock Creek, Lowman, ID 208 259 3740
swansont@mac.com

A sincere thank you for purchasing my new book,
Graduation: "So What Just Happened?"

Tom Brokaw once said, *"It's easy to make a buck,
it is much harder to make a difference!"*

My hope and prayer is that this book will make a difference in the life of every reader. Successful application would make me more satisfied than just a few laughs and enjoyment.

Always keep your chin up, but keep your nose at a friendly level!

It would be appreciated if you would write a short review or recommendation. The few words of a satisfied reader are most helpful. I would love to feature some of them in the next printing of this book, or in my other promotions. Please send them to swansont@mac.com.

Your ideas, thoughts, reflections and suggestions would be most welcome. To make my writings more helpful to the readers is what I desire.

Be bold in what you stand for: be careful for what you fall for!

To get a personalized, autographed copy email the name and your mailing address at: swansont@mac.com

The fastest way to get another copy is to go directly to my printer [they print on demand] at:
https://www.createspace.com/4243539

To close, I hope you are encouraged by the book, and here is another sincere thank you.

*I kept wondering why the baseball was getting bigger......
Then it hit me!*

"AHA!" SECTION 6

So, How Will You Know If You Are Making Progress?

Be encouraged! Think how far you have already come. If you are a graduate, congratulate yourself. Everyone should congratulate himself or herself on having arrived at this point in life. You have accomplishments worth remembering. The lessons learned, either the hard or easy way, will prepare you as you continue on to your next steps.

Remember pilgrim, there is no path;
the path is made by walking.

So, what's this thing called progress? Very simply, progress is moving in a positive, constructive direction. Ask yourself if you are doing that? You must first set the direction and then monitor and evaluate your progress.

Clarifying your expectations is the first step. Whether you call them goals or objectives, what do you want to see happen next? Listing your goals on paper often helps. Organize the different areas of your life and develop word pictures of what you want your future to look like.

Vision: your description of a preferred future.

Take an evaluating look at those expectations. Are they reality based? What are the realistic possibilities that they can be accomplished in a timely, orderly fashion? Can you make them happen within your present situation? Are you setting yourself up for failure?

A major part of the growing up process is to choose and determine your goals. Where did you get this vision of your preferred future? If they came from your parents, some book or magazine, the internet, your friends, or any other source, *are they really yours?* You will have to invest everything you have to achieve them. Do you really believe they will be worth all your effort and investment? Remember, it will be your time, money, and effort being invested. Make them *your* goals.

Did you plan to fail,
or fail to plan?

Some destinations, or expectations, are "crazy-makers." Your subconscious is a committed servant who will strive to accomplish any goal, no matter how impossible or "crazy." Choose wisely. Don't destroy yourself in the process.

"AHA!" SECTION 6

You have always wanted a certain kind of a very unique hat. Finally, you find it! "Crazy-makers" are when you buy this unique, expensive hat at a great price (oh, by the way, the hat is the wrong size). You then spend the rest of your life trying to adjust your head to fit the hat.

Wisdom is the ability to effectively evaluate decisions before you start the process. What will be the total costs of the project, and will the results be a predictable success?

At some point you have become like the sea captain—in order to reach your destination, you have to leave the safety of the harbor and venture out into the open seas. Bon voyage!

Be encouraged! You are on your way. You have made a statement with your actions. You are now committed!

***To reach a goal you have never attained,
expect to do things you have never done before.***

Since you have committed to your goals and action plan, you have them firmly in your mind. Be confident as you move out. Doubt will be the enemy, but frequent spot-checks will restore your resolve. Remember: ***I will be the best me I can be!***

A very important part of your action plan must be your timeline. How long will each part of your journey take? Periodic checkpoints will prove valuable in evaluating your progress.

Most journeys will have a cost-benefit factor. Have you intelligently planned for all the various types of costs that will be needed for completion? Monitoring the supplies and costs must be one of your highest priorities in checking your progress.

Your mind-set must constantly be evaluating: *Is what you're doing activity or productivity?* The wisdom to know the difference is really important.

It is very easy to get caught up in the speed of the journey. How many times as a little kid did you ask your parents, *"Are we there yet?"* A firm grasp on your timeline, and checking where you are currently, will bring sanity to the progress.

Keep in mind that life is always a work in progress, moving satisfactorily in right direction. I like this reminder: *Often the difference between try and triumph is a little "umph."* Every day will take more focused effort.

Making progress implies movement towards a desired end. Having a well thought out process for measuring progress must be a constant traveling partner. I remembering smiling when I heard,

> *When you get to top of the ladder is a bad time to realize the ladder is leaning against the wrong building!*

I hope you have been a lifelong student of leadership. Valuable lessons can be learned from the lives of leaders who have succeeded, as well as those who have failed. You now have the opportunity and responsibility for your life and progress.

Be encouraged! You must lead yourself before you can lead others. Your philosophy of how to treat other people will be a

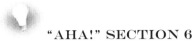

major part in your success. Being assertive and strong, while always having a win-win attitude, is the hallmark of most successful leaders.

Hopefully you do not have an "instant success" factor in your game plan. Expect to have to solve problems and make adjustments. Even the best laid plans are a set of ideas leading into the future that will always run smack dab into reality. There are no foolproof, perfect plans. *Life is: adjust!*

The more quickly you can sense something is wrong, get the facts of reality, develop adjustments and solutions, and get things back on track, will help you become a better, problem-solving leader.

If at first you don't succeed, welcome to the club.

One mark of progress is consistently evaluating your game plan. Just like that postage stamp, stick to your plan until you succeed. Remember the fish that didn't know about the hook? Try to avoid the temptation to check out those shiny, new distractions. The hook might get you.

Carefully select your "should and ought" statements! If they move you along your road of success, agree and carry on. Avoid distracting, defeating self-talk.

Did you make today matter, about things that really matter?

On your journey to success, the novelty and excitement of starting your journey will fade. It will not be new and interesting every day. It rapidly turns into good old hard work. Learn some new tricks to deal with the drudgery of keeping focused on hard work.

Be encouraged! Fatigue makes cowards of all of us. It takes courage and resolve to show up with your work boots on and your energy tank full. Often the long journey will seem longer. When you get weary, it takes extra mental and emotional focus to stay on task. Long distance drivers always have to battle highway hypnosis.

Always proofread carefully to see if you any words out.

One is often tempted to adjust reality with words. *Saying so won't make it so.* Excuses will be understood as excuses. Your word must be your bond, both to yourself and others. Your actions and results will always speak louder and clearer than your words.

Formula for success: Under-promise and over-deliver.

Perfection is an imposter that always will show up on the job site and start offering suggestions, which are always criticism. If you are the leader, and leader of your team, get rid of Mr. Perfection instantly.

Be encouraged! Keep your eye on the prize, and your foot on the pedal. Because of your wise planning and problem-solving execution, you will start to see the light at the end of the tunnel.

Way to go! You have earned your *"Congratulations!*

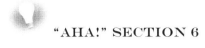

Success

Success is never final; failure is seldom fatal.

Now it gets a little tricky. Success has been defined in a multitude of ways. In the greater world of success, how will you arrive at your definition of personal success?

Just like it's unreasonable to adjust to wearing someone else's clothes, so be careful that your goals are your goals. Others can subtly influence your choice. Parents, grandparents, siblings, friends, and your views of all kinds of successful people can plant seeds in your mind.

Make sure your goals reflect your deepest values. When your core values reinforce your effort and goals, it is a lot easier to get up and get going each morning. You are building and investing in success that you really value deep down inside.

Imagine your future as a parade celebrating your successful journey to completion. It would be a lot more enjoyable with everything coming together smoothly. The more factors you can efficiently bring together will produce a harmonious process.

Be encouraged! You can define success on your terms. Your life's accomplishments can bear witness to your character, values, and how you accomplished your purposes.

**Failure waits for those who stay
with some success made yesterday.**

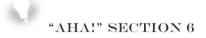

The Triangle of Success

Always play the angles: use the "try-angle!"

Seems like everyone is looking for some angle, trick, or the latest guru for the secrets of success. In the next "aha" insights we will focus on an interesting model. No secrets or angles, just something visual, solid, and effective.

This model is not my creation; so big thanks to the unknown author, because I really like it. *The Triangle of Success* is built on 1. Strong Thought, 2. Dynamic Action, 3. Honest Evaluation. Simple, straightforward, direct, and "right on!"

Travelers use road maps, architects use blue prints, and this can be your model for success. Gathering, organizing, research will all prove beneficial to your success. Using this model can help you organize and stay focused on success.

Knowledge, application, and execution will bring the *Triangle of Success* model to life. The devil is often in the details, but by having an organizational system, you can find the flaws through good evaluation. Time is a-wasting, let's get going.

Be encouraged! You can organize and execute a successful endeavor. Strong Thought, Dynamic Action, and Honest Evaluation will guide your successful journey.

The Tri-angle of Success: Try! Try! Try!

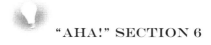

Strong Thought

Plan the Work: Work the Plan

Vision has been defined as your view of a preferred future. Your vision of success is a must. Strong thought starts with a realistic view of what your want to successfully accomplish.

A realistic view of the assets you bring to your project is significant. What will you be able to bring to the project? Fantasy must be conditioned with your rational and realistic approach.

Every successful project is a combination of successful planning to give purpose and direction to the execution. Every set of blueprints, every game plan, every financial plan, every business plan is the first step in strong thought. Anticipation and preparation are key ingredients of strong thought.

Dynamic action must also have a strong thought component. What timing and what actions will come together to produce success. Many plans fail when activity without strong thought overrides productive behaviors.

Be encouraged! Strong thought will produce great accomplishments. Investing in organizing your strong thoughts will pay great dividends throughout the project or journey.

The strongest chain is as strong as its weakest "think!"

Dynamic Action

Don't just do something: Stand There!

Do you see your life as basically green lights or red lights? Some folks always jump the gun and speed ahead out of control. Others seem stuck at the red light, waiting………..

It's great to have a full tank of gas for your trip. But, you get an explosion when throwing gas on a fire. It's far better to run that fuel through a smooth running engine.

Dynamic Action is intense, direct energy into purposeful, productive behavior. You have carefully prepared your action plan to accomplish your vision of a preferred future. Everything is coming together to reach your destination.

The excitement and novelty of starting on a long journey will always wear off. Expect to quickly arrive at the stage of hard, disciplined *work*! Determined effort, often approaching fatigue, is the price that has to be paid for significant, meaningful accomplishments.

Be encouraged! Your strong thoughts have produced a vision worthy of your efforts. Faithful, committed effort will pay off upon completion of your project or journey.

Don't shoot your mouth off before your brain is loaded.

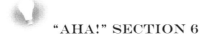

Honest Evaluation
Is what you are doing activity, or productivity?

Becoming preoccupied with your project, getting lost in the details is often what happens. You have your head down, working hard, putting in countless hours, until……. Did you forget to stop and check your progress, making sure you are proceeding in the right direction?

It is always super important to keep the big picture in mind, making sure you know your current location within the project. *It is a lot easier to stay out of trouble, than to get out of trouble!* Frequent stops at check-points is a very valuable behavior!

So, how do we honestly evaluate our progress? First, reflect on whether you can do an effective job on your own? Second, how do you select independent outsiders to give you trusted input?

I have learned I don't do a very good job proof reading my own work. Another set of eyes has proven to be most valuable. Even with the best of intentions, only trusted outsiders can be objective.

Be encouraged! It is worth the time and effort to establish an effective, timely evaluation process. Better to evaluate as the project unfolds, correct as you go, instead of experiencing the disappointment of project failure.

Don't be so busy you forget to take time to sharpen your axe!

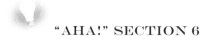

Ready! Set! Go!
Perfect aim is useless unless you pull the trigger!

One of the greatest secrets of world class target shooting is to calm your breathing and heart rate. Anticipation, excitement, and adrenaline are normal ingredients in the launch of something important. Something is missing if you are not *"pumped,"* or whatever today's word is for super excited.

If it's important you always do it scared! Understanding that truth, you get your emotions under control. A smooth, consistent delivery of your energy over the long term is a super significant part of success.

The *Triangle of Success* must be an equilateral triangle, meaning each of the three ideas is equally important. Planning, execution, and timely evaluation builds a successful project. You must continually handle the process, and progress.

A lack of planning and execution on your part does not make an emergency on someone else's part. The call to action, the start of the event, implies you are the driver of this project. You assume the leadership mantle for this operation's success.

Be encouraged! There is a world of successful projects you can use as an encouraging model. Focused attention to each of the *Triangle of Success* principles will have you properly prepared. *Ready! Set! Go!*

Some folks would rather look at the map than actually visit the place.

Coffee Break!

"Let's Try Not To Strain Your Brain."

A morning without coffee is like sleep.

Remember this on your next birthday:
Rumor has it: Happy Birthday. As Kermit the frog says, "Time's fun when you're having flies!" Enjoy but don't let the "fun-o-meter" go off. Isn't this the oldest you have ever been? Remember, the more birthdays you have, the longer you live. The main thing is to keep the main thing the main thing.

I'd stop drinking coffee, but I'm no quitter.

Conversation is like Ping-Pong:
The ball must keep going back and forth across the net to have a game!

He Who Laughs: Lasts!

"AHA!" SECTION 7

Are You Ready for the Final Exam?
No, I Mean Life's "Final Final"!

There is something final about the word final. Final carries with it a huge implication that "good-news" or "bad- news" is coming. Final makes one seriously consider positive benefits, or unwelcome consequences. Final really creates an approach-avoidance conflict.

In the world of academics, athletics, negotiations, and courtroom proceedings, competitive folks know that the final decision or verdict determines the winner. The old ABC Wild World of Sports TV show coined the phrase, *"the thrill of victory, and the agony of defeat."* Real competitors strive for success.

Likewise in another perspective, some folks understand the serious consequences of failing instead of passing, guilty instead of innocent, free instead of fines or jail time. Realizing the consequence of the final verdict—that the future might be significantly more difficult—brings an ominous sense of potential dread while awaiting the outcome.

Understanding the idea that there is a *Final Final* at the end of your life provides you with a lifetime of preparation. Since it will be your *Final Final,* serious consideration and reflection would prove valuable. One word of caution, **the end of life often arrives early and unannounced.** Being prepared *"sooner instead of later"* might be wise counsel.

Reality is the leading cause of stress!

Navigating life between success and failure really is stressful. On many days, the carefree days of childhood bring back nostalgic memories. Why can't being an adult be the same as our childhood? Reality very quickly forces us into dealing with our adult situations in an adult manner.

Looking across the cultural landscape, we see a very wide spectrum of philosophies. The self reliant, rugged individual stresses that you are the champion of your success, or the creator of your failures. *Man up! Grow up!*

The other extreme wants to make excuses and blame anyone or everyone, anything or everything, for the difficult situations that arise. These folks feel they are entitled to the good life that society should provide for them.

Victimhood has an attraction where we are not responsible, and someone else should provide the solution to our problem. Whatever operational philosophy one has, there will be positive or negative consequences. With every choice comes benefits or outcomes we will have to continue to endure.

If you don't change directions, you'll end up where you're going.

Monitoring your choices and your progress is a sign of maturity. Knowing your location on your journey through life is expected. Assessing your progress in a positive, or negative direction is your responsibility. *It's your life to live.*

Life comes with no guarantees. Just like the weather, our lives can be bright, sunny and very pleasant, or the storms of life seem overwhelming. *Life is; adjust and deal with it!* Accepting individual responsibility is a sign of maturity.

While I have no solution, I do admire your problem.

Have you ever reflected on which is more important — *questions or answers?* Having an answer that doesn't fit the question is a waste of time. Having questions that don't pertain to your situation are equally useless. Important, focused questions, that guide our search for satisfactory answers, are very valuable.

In life we have daily issues, problems, and challenges that seem to take over the agenda. *The urgent overwhelms the important.* We often have to major in the minor things of life. It often is quite easy to fall back on our excuses.

The road to failure is often paved with good intentions.

One of the characteristics in defining life is the *"will to live."* There are fantastically amazing stories of individuals overcoming almost insurmountable odds to make it out alive. Strength of character and resolve are the stuff of which heroes are made.

I remember watching Lassie, a TV show about a collie that always was able to overcome the situation and be successful. My wise older brother reminded me that Lassie had to be successful because Lassie *had to succeed* so he could be on next week's show.

Life is not always that way. Tragedy, difficulty, and even death come knocking on our door. Somehow we continue to believe that we will escape the bad news and continue to live happily ever after just like the fairy tales.

Death is a subject that we often avoid in our living, thinking, and conversation. It is important to realize that the death statistics are very impressive: one out of one people die. Someone has said that the interesting thing about life is that nobody gets out of life alive.

While checking the obituaries might sound a little morbid, the lesson to be learned is that people pass away, and at any age. Average statistics give little comfort. When death comes, it is always perceived as arriving early.

Hope is the feeling that the feeling you have isn't permanent.

At some point in your life, or in the lives of those closest to you, the *Final Final* question must be considered. *Your life has now ended, what will happen next?*

"AHA!" SECTION 7

An interesting insight to realize is that your life is now over, and you cannot actively participate in the answering the question at that point. Death demands you make your preparations and arrangements while you are still alive.

Also, on your journey through life, you have not been able to observe or experience exactly what happens to other people after they have passed away. It becomes a lonely prospect that you alone have to face this *Final Final* experience. Your eternal future will hang in the balance. It really becomes the *Final Final!*

The following *"aha"* sections will provide insights and questions to challenge your thinking. How does one get ready for the *Final Final?*

The perspectives on life after death, or eternal life, have a very wide spectrum. Those on one end say, *"Your life is over, done and finished! You don't have to deal with life anymore."* Your story has ended.

On the other end of that spectrum they say everyone will face spending eternal life someplace: Heaven or Hell. The implications of considering that wide a continuum present everyone with a serious challenge in preparing for your *Final Final*.

Since you individually will experience your *Final Final* results, your preparation takes on a much greater importance. Some suggest that our entire life is spent trying to get to God, to impress God, to get God to like us more. You are encouraged to seriously reconsider that suggestion.

I'm not OK! You're not OK! But, that's OK!

In the Christmas story in Luke 2:10, the Christmas angel reassured them, *"'Don't be afraid,' he said, 'I bring good news that will bring great joy to all people!'"*

The basic tenet of understanding Jesus Christ is that eternal life is a gift. You cannot earn a gift. You are encouraged to desire that gift, to ask for that gift, unwrap that gift and put the gift into use where you will benefit greatly. The most significant part of the gift is a lifetime warranty and guarantee: it is good for this life, and the next. This gift is the only gift with a guarantee and warranty that never ends, assured and validated by God Himself!

With that new perspective, your view of your Final Final can significantly change. As the Apostle Paul said about his *Final Final*, *"for me to live is Jesus Christ, and to die is gain!"* With this kind of optimism and confidence, *"Sign me up!"*

It was a really good day;
I got a lot of serious procrastination done!

While considering the next seven "aha!" ideas, time might be of the essence. ***"Not to decide is to decide!"*** It is my goal and prayer that you will seriously consider your preparation for your *Final Final*. Sometimes being asked a significant and serious question is a life-changing gift. Carry on.

Your "Final Final" !

I intend to live forever; so far, so good.
Steven Wright

At some point in your life, hopefully sooner than later, I hope you will take a look at your own mortality. There is plenty of light-hearted humor about death and the unknown after life. It would be sad to be unprepared when the end of your life arrives.

I would expect that you have had someone say, *"As my friend, why didn't you tell me?"* None of us is smart enough to know and be prepared for everything on the journey through life. My prayer is that you have those kind of friends who care enough to help you keep up to speed on the big, important things of life.

One of my mentors told me to keep asking questions, *not* to control the answer, *but* to control the question. A gift of the proper question, at the appropriate time, should be welcomed, and treasured. A true friend should care about your eternal well-being.

Be encouraged! The major, life-influencing answers to the major questions of life must be your answer. My concern is that you will have been presented with those super important questions.

I'm sure you know that death will knock on your door someday. My prayer is that you have come to some firm conclusions, based on wise and true information. You eternity rests on what you decide.

Many books inform you; only the Bible transforms you.

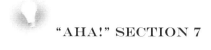

Jesus
Who is This Man? John Ortberg

I would guess that at some point in your life you have asked the question, *"Who is that person?"* For some reason, you are curious or intrigued by that someone. You just had to find out more.

I remember the first time I saw my wife Donna. I was young and asked my dad, *"Who is that girl?"* I'm really glad I asked, and as Paul Harvey always said, *"Now you know the rest of the story!"*

John Ortberg titled his new book, *"Who is This Man?"* John goes on to inform us how Jesus confronted the Jewish, Roman, and Greek power base of the culture of His time and completely changed it. If you take time to read this book you will have to answer the question, *"REALLY, who was/is this man Jesus?"*

Bill O'Reilly has just released his new book, *"Who killed Jesus?"* in time for Easter. Bill asks a really interesting question, *"How did Jesus have such a tremendous influence on his culture and history, without a power base?"* He started out with nothing but himself.

Jesus brought the "Gospel" to mankind. What was this life-changing "good news" Jesus proclaimed and taught? At some point in your life, I believe this question will become eternally important for you to have answered correctly.

Where would the world be today if Jesus had quit before he got His work done?

Jesus - Liar?

To you, I am an atheist: to God, I'm the loyal opposition.
Woody Allen

C.S Lewis, once an agnostic and a world famous professor at Cambridge University, commented, "Considering what Jesus said and taught, you must make a choice: either this man Jesus was, and is, the Son of God; or else a madman or something worse." With that powerful a statement, *"Who is this Jesus he is talking about?"*

Josh McDowell also started out as an agnostic or atheist. The story of his search to understand Jesus is told in his book, *"More than a Carpenter."* Josh concluded Jesus is either a liar, a lunatic, or Lord! This choice is the choice every one of us must make because of the eternal nature of this man Jesus.

Jesus got in trouble with the Jewish leaders because he claimed to be God, and He forgave sin. That infuriated the Jewish religious leaders who believed that *only* God could forgive sin, and Jesus had the arrogance and audacity to make that claim.

Jesus made this statement, **"I am the way, the truth, and the life. No one can come to the Father except through me."** [John 14:6] Interesting, powerful and controversial statement: "*The* way, *The* truth, and *The* life... *No One...*" Really, who does this young teacher think he is?

Be encouraged! It sounds quite probable that this guy could be a liar. He made some unbelievable statements. Listening to Paul Harvey, maybe you'd better check out the rest of the Jesus story?

Aspire to inspire before you expire!

111

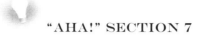

Jesus - Lunatic?

How young can you be to die from old age?
Steven Wright

We all know some people who are very sincere, and very sincerely wrong. The intensity and sincerity of your belief does not make it right. Truth determines correctness.

There was a heated argument in the mental ward. One man claimed to be Moses and was asked, "Who told you that?" He proudly answered, "God did," and immediately there followed a loud reply from across the room, "I Did Not!"

Anyone can say anything, but you must be ready to meet the critics and the skeptics. Most of us were not born yesterday and have heard plenty of fishy sounding stories. Good mental health always has a little skepticism ready to check things out.

The more you read of the Jesus story in the New Testament of the Bible, the more you are presented with an amazing, fantastic story. This man Jesus said many things sounding unbelievable to us humans. At times, one must question whether he was telling the truth, or was he really delusional?

Be encouraged! You can read the whole story for yourself. Nothing is hidden or left out. The most encouraging part of reading for yourself is that God's Holy Spirit will help you with the understanding of the Truth.

Not to decide is to decide!

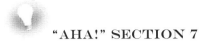

Jesus – Lord?

He is no fool who gives up what he cannot keep,
to gain what he cannot lose. Jim Elliot

Most of us had parents who were sneaky, and a little quicker than us. As youngsters they were always offering us choices. You can have this, or that, but not both. They never let us add a third option.

Josh McDowell offers us three choices about Jesus: *liar, lunatic or Lord.* Can you think of another alternative? It would be nice not to have to make a forced choice.

In one of the previous "Aha" insights, I asked you to think about your life equation for success. I suggested the importance of considering a God or Jesus factor being in your personal equation. Have you made that decision and already put it into practice?

We attended a Christmas service in a new town one Christmas morning, and realized we were in the wrong church. Being too embarrassed to get up and walk out, we stayed. The pastor gave the *best* Christmas message: *"Did you leave the Jesus Package unwrapped under your tree?"*

Be encouraged, because of the change in my life, and seeing it in so many people, in so many countries, I believe Jesus is who He claimed to be, both Savior and Lord. I cannot make that decision for you, only you can. The New Testament tells the whole story of Jesus, with the power of His Holy Spirit to help you understand the truth.

Preach the Gospel of Jesus Christ every day; use words only when necessary. St. Augustine

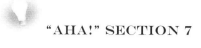

Sin

I don't smoke, and I don't chew, and I don't go with the girls who do!

The old country preacher started his Sunday sermon, *"I reckon there's a whole lot of sinnin' goin' on around here!"* Most kids believed their moms, dads, and ministers had ganged up on them with a *huge* list of "no-no's." Their goal was to take all the fun out of growing up.

Sin has always been a controversial subject, in every culture, in every age. Every religion has a list of suggested positive behaviors and a list of behaviors that are taboo. Sin is often the name of that category of prohibited behaviors.

Growing up, I came face to face with the list of *"no, can't, and don't ever get caught doing!"* The game became coming up with a plan to do it, but not getting caught. We believed it was *okay* if we got away with it.

Later my thinking came around to the idea, shouldn't one be focusing on doing the right or positive things, instead of things to avoid? It made more sense to me to make a list of "Do's" instead of "Don'ts." Jesus really came to teach and demonstrate a positive message of thinking and behaving.

My current definition of Sin is more of an attitude that says, *"Thanks, but no thanks, I don't need, or want God in my life; I'm doing just fine on my own."* There is never any agreement on the prohibited behaviors, but remember Jesus said, *"Come, follow Me, and I will…."* [Mark 1:17]

It's often a lot easier to get forgiveness than permission.

See You at the House?

When something is dead and gone, only a resurrection will bring it back.
John Fischer

Jim was a dear friend confined to a hospital bed the last three to four years of his life. He had a small white board propped up for visitors to read:

1. Please wake me if I'm sleeping, and
2. *"I'll see you at the House!"* He included it in every conversation, asking if his visitor knew to what the second point referred.

Jesus said, *"In my Father's house are many rooms. If it were not so, would I have told you that I go to prepare a place for you?"* [John 14:2] If the visitor knew what Jim was referring to, they would celebrate spending eternity together. If they didn't, Jim would say he would be praying for them, and would ask if they would like to learn more about Heaven.

At the passing away of a friend, or at their funeral, I often hear, *"I'm so happy because they are now in a better place."* The reality is that this might not be so. Jesus said Heaven is only reserved for those who have believed in Him and have acknowledged Him as their Savior and Lord. Jesus says in John 3:15 [the verse just before the most famous verse in the Bible], *"so that anyone who believes in me will have eternal life."* When Jesus speaks, it is best to listen!

Jesus and the Bible speak clearly about a life after death, for eternity. Heaven is a gathering place for all those who have claimed the gift of salvation, and the new life Jesus offers. Since this is Jesus's residence, he has set up the process and procedures for admission:

1. Those who have asked Jesus to forgive their sins,

2. Those who have asked Jesus into their lives,

3. Those who have asked Jesus to make them into people like Jesus, and

4.Those who tell their friends they have accepted Jesus as their Savior and Lord will be welcomed by Jesus into Heaven.

Jesus will give you new life in this world starting now, and for eternity. You can't earn this gift of eternal life; just accept the love, forgiveness, and gift of His salvation offered by Jesus.

Be encouraged! Jesus is already listening. Just ask Him and then start following and rejoicing. *"Ask and you will receive."* [Matt. 7:7]

"Everybody talkin' 'bout Heaven ain't goin' there!"
[Old Negro Spiritual]

Let me conclude with the perspective Dr. James Allen gave to a group of young people in Los Angeles, California in 1926. It has become one of the best descriptions of the impact Jesus had on the world. Have you personalized that impact into your life and eternal future?

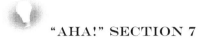

One Solitary Life

He was born in an obscure village. The child of a peasant woman, He grew up in another obscure village, where he worked in a carpenter shop until he was thirty. He never wrote a book. He never held an office. He never went to college. He never visited a big city. He never travelled more than two hundred miles from the place where he was born. He did none of the things usually associated with greatness. He had no credentials but himself.

He was only thirty-three, his friends ran away. One of them denied him. He was turned over to his enemies, and went through the mockery of a trial. He was nailed to a cross between two thieves. While dying, his executioners gambled for his clothing, the only property he had on earth. When he was dead, He was laid in a borrowed grave, through the pity of a friend.

*Nineteen centuries have come and gone, and today Jesus is the central figure of the human race, and the leader of mankind's progress. All the armies that have ever marched, all the navies that have ever sailed, all the parliaments that have ever sat, all the kings that ever reigned put together have not affected the life of mankind on earth as powerfully as **that one solitary life**.*

Dr. James Allan © 1926.

You are invited to finalize your answer: *"Who do you say Jesus Christ is in your life and future?*

So...

Time for a "pop quiz"!

Remember how you hated those infamous "pop quizzes"? As a student, I remember checking in with other students who were leaving class if there were any surprises in class that day. Nobody likes to be caught unprepared.

In a certain way, life is a daily "pop quiz." As every day arrives early, unannounced and right on time, you can never guess what surprises each day could bring. Is today going to be a "pop quiz" day?

I am a volunteer ambulance driver in our mountain community. When the tone-out from Idaho State Communication sounds, it is expected that I immediately drop everything and respond. Those we are called to help have already had their "pop quiz" of life and need our immediate help.

My dad, Lester Swanson, had an interesting way of responding to me. Often when I came with an idea, feeling or situation, he would pause, think, and very often would respond with, "So?" In the surprise "pop quizzes" of life, no one else can take the quiz for you.

As we end our time together, thanks for hanging in there. Whether it is just a daily "pop quiz," or your *Final Final* has arrived, Jesus really wants you to succeed. Jesus and His Holy Spirit have been continually encouraging you to learn and be ready; hopefully, you are fully prepared.

Just wondering, is today The Day?

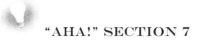

Encore!

"Do 'gain, Grandpa. Do 'gain!"

At the end of an enjoyable music concert, the crowd often gives loud and continuous applause. They hope their enthusiastic response will bring the performers back for another song or two. Let's keep this enjoyable evening going.

> It was Caleb's first firework's show. He was sitting, entranced, in my lap, watching intently. All of a sudden, it was over and dark. I then heard this little, quiet voice say so sweetly, **"Do 'gain, Grandpa. Do 'gain!"** Even a little guy hoped for an encore.

As an encore, I would like to share a column that was very instrumental in my growing understanding of the person and role of Jesus. Dr. Lloyd Ahlem gives a light-hearted, humorous insight to the wisdom and truths of Jesus Christ. Enjoy, learn, and be blessed:

A CHRISTIAN MANIFESTO FOR PEOPLE WHO DO NOT LIKE BIG WORDS

God is in charge of everything. He began it all and he will end it all. How he goes about it is somewhat confusing but very interesting. You can get a lot of college and seminary degrees trying to figure it all out.

God thinks he is self-evident. He is not too worried about your proving whether or not he exists. Simple people can find out a lot about him without much hassle of the brain.

God loves people. He turned himself into a man so he could be like you. He had babyhood, colic, wet pants, adolescent trauma, manhood, and divinity. It is the strangest combination you have ever heard of. He is called Jesus. This combination will not fit any of your notions about what God ought to be like.

Through the years God got some people to write down what they learned about him. The used their own words and descriptions as best they could. They did very well because we can find out about him even today, and the words tell the truth. A lot of people argue about the words, but their fussing is not very important.

God has the best forgetter in the universe. He knows you screw up your life and make a lot of booboos. Knowing what you are like he decided to forgive you for being normal, before you ever got started goofing. That way the heat is off you and on him. You can forget about feeling guilty for all your nonsense unless you decide to be your own God and fix everything yourself. Many people do this. It is very tiring. There is always somebody to apologize to, some stupid act to rationalize, and some dumb mistake that cannot be corrected. After a while you will not give a care. You will either let God forgive you the way he wants to or you will go on getting

more guilt and not fixing any of it. But fortunately Jesus paid all our moral and spiritual bills and you do not have to contribute a thing — just accept the gift.

Since God has no memory of your klutzy deeds or seamy motives, he likes what he sees in you. He enjoys your company. He laughs and sings and dances when you come around. He is like a father who wants to do more for you than you can imagine. He tries not to be too indulgent because you might get spoiled. So you may not get everything your wishes desire. God is not half as hard on you as people are. He loves so much he will forgive stuff most Christian people would like to hold you accountable for. Do not worry about those people. They will get tired of it and start forgiving when their energies run down. Try copying God when it comes to forgiving yourself. You are probably tougher on yourself than he is, too!

God will give your life direction and meaning. Just start doing the things that show love to people and let God put all you do into a pattern. By loving and serving you will discover your abilities and God will expand your opportunities. A lot of books have been written on special, secret, mysterious, and unusual ways to dig out what God has in mind for people. Ignore most of these and read the New Testament. Then do only the things that do not confuse you.

Sing a lot, worship a lot, hope a lot and remember God must have a sense of humor to make the likes of you. He always has a surprise when he moves you along in your life. He is never completely predictable. Serendipity is always in his mind. Accept it with cheer.

"AHA!" SECTION 7

Someday you will get to live in his house. All those people who decided to be their own god will get to live alone with their god too. Living with God will be so attractive you will likely dump every other hope into lesser priority. This will be true even if Social Security runs out. Neither the Democrats nor Republicans are in charge of the final outcome of things.

Enjoy! God loves you and has paid your way!

by Lloyd Ahlem
Originally printed in
"The Covenant Companion."

Coffee Break!

"Let's Try Not To Strain Your Brain."

Coffee smells like freshly ground heaven.

Dear God: Big Ocean, little boat. Help!

All the coffee in Columbia won't
make me a morning person.

*"Don't feel totally, personally,
irrevocably, eternally responsible for
everything. That's my job."*
Love,
GOD

He Who Laughs: Lasts!

So, Why Should You Be Encouraged?

Welcome to the end of **GRADUATION: "So, What Just Happened?** Do you remember *the adventure begins where the road ends?* Maybe we now need to think about *"where the book ends."*

Welcome to the world of your growing independence. To become a fully functioning adult, you need to keep becoming more responsible and independent. I think you really do want to be driving your own life to *your* success.

The road to failure is often paved with good intentions.

It might be good start, but intentions need to be turned into *"attentions."* You must attend and implement your action steps.

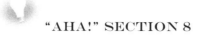

Saying so won't make it so!

Realistic optimism needs to become your constant traveling companion. Tremendous possibilities await you. You have built for yourself a solid foundation on which to build your dreams.

We all are a work in progress.

Progress is a process verb. Breathing, walking, hoping are not *"one and done"* activities. You must keep on doing. Keep connecting the progress of each minute, hour, and day, and you will be greatly encouraged by your movement towards success.

Be encouraged! Make your purposeful behaviors into dynamic habits of willful accomplishments. You are building and making your future. You are guaranteed to spend 100% of your future with yourself. Make a fantastic future for yourself and others.

Bad habits are like a comfortable bed, easy to get into, but hard to get out of.

Respect your humanity. You cannot and never will achieve perfection, so forgive yourself for being human and become your own best cheerleader. *It might be nice to be important, but it is more important to be nice,* especially to yourself.

To err is human; that's why the eraser wears out before the pencil.

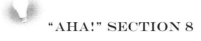

"AHA!" SECTION 8

We are often tempted to justify our mistakes and try to cover them over. It is amazing how creative our rationalizations can become. I remind myself to stay out of trouble so that I don't have to figure out how to get myself out of trouble. Make good decisions on the front end.

An ounce of preparation is worth a pound of cure.

Be encouraged! Watch out for your self-talk. Talk yourself into the best things, and out of the things you should avoid. Be especially careful about your "shoulds" and "oughts." You can become your best friend or your worst enemy.

I have really enjoyed writing **GRADUATION:** *"So, what just happened?"* While writing, I have been thinking of my daughters and grandkids, so many students from 35 years of teaching and coaching, and so many fantastic, life-long friends from our Young Life family, both in the United States and in eight countries of the former Soviet Union. My goal and prayer always was, and still is, that I might be able to help every reader to have a better and a more enjoyable and purposeful life.

Few of these one-liners are my creation. Again, a sincere thank you to all the original authors. Your insights have become the *"wisdom of the common man."* As these one-liners have helped me on my travels through life, may they help you, and please pass them out freely to assist your fellow travelers. All of us are smarter than one of us.

If you do not go after what you want,
expect to never have it!

"AHA!" SECTION 8

It is incredible the blessing my family, students and friends have been to me. I constantly thank the Good Lord for His provision and blessing. Being blessed, or lucky, is a serious understatement. Thanks to all who have brought so much joy and laughter into my life. May you become a gracious and thankful blessing to all those you travel with on your life's journey.

So here is wishing, and praying, that you will have a fantastic, successful journey for yourself, and all those you can help to achieve a better future. One of my deepest prayers is that you will be perfectly prepared for your *Final Final*. Then we can laugh and tell stories for eternity. Always remember: Love, Hugs, and Prayers from Grandpa Tom!

Live simply. Love generously. Care deeply.
Speak kindly. Leave the rest to God.

"AHA!" SECTION 8

You are invited. . .

Contact "Professor OB1 Kaswanni":

If you have been doing some serious reflection about the thoughts about Jesus and learning about following Jesus, I would love to visit with you. I can be contacted at **swansont@mac.com** and we can keep in touch by email or I would be happy to call you "on my dime." Looking forward to visiting.
(Also, an autographed copy of GRADUATION: "So, What Just Happened?" can be ordered by using this information.)

Tom Swanson
38 Rock Creek Dr.
Lowman, ID 83637
(208) 259-3740
swansont@mac.com

Tom and Donna Swanson boarding train at Chernivtski, Ukraine

Tom and Donna with Young Life leadership team in
Ararat, Armenia

Proceeds from sales of **GRADUATION: *"So, What Just Happened?"*** will help fund travel for Tom and Donna to befriend, encourage and train Young Life leaders across the former Soviet Union. Young Life is a friendship building outreach ministry to share the "good news" of Jesus.

Tom and Donna have made 12 trips, paying their own way, to Armenia, Georgia, Kazakhstan, Kyrgyzstan, Moldova, Russia, and Ukraine. They try to take two trips a year to help leaders grow in their love of Jesus, become better friends with young people, and find and train new leaders to grow the Young Life ministry in their countries.

Young Life leadership team in Zaporishia, Ukraine

Bibliography

More Than a Carpenter, Josh McDowell. Tyndale House, Living Books Edition (1973).

A Choice of Kipling's Verse Made By T.S. Eliot with an Essay on Rudyard Kipling. Charles Scribner's Sons; First Edition (1943).

Who Is This Man: The Unpredictable Impact of the Inescapable Jesus, John Ortberg. Zondervan (August 7, 2012).

The 7 Habits of Highly Effective People, Stephen R. Covey. Free Press. Revised edition (November 9, 2004).

When Riding a Dead Horse, for Heavens Sake...Dismount! Barry Asmus. Ameripress (March 1995).

The Secret of Staying in Love, John Powell. Thomas More. Reprint edition (December 1995).

"One Solitary Life," Dr. James Allan Francis. From his book *The Real Jesus and Other Sermons.* The Judson Press (1926).

Called to Be Friends, Paula Ripple. Ave Maria Press (1982).

Growing Slowly Wise — Building a Faith that Works, David Roper. Discovery House Publishers (August, 2000).